1 MONTH OF FREE READING

at

www.ForgottenBooks.com

By purchasing this book you are eligible for one month membership to ForgottenBooks.com, giving you unlimited access to our entire collection of over 1,000,000 titles via our web site and mobile apps.

To claim your free month visit:
www.forgottenbooks.com/free174653

* Offer is valid for 45 days from date of purchase. Terms and conditions apply.

ISBN 978-0-266-56970-1
PIBN 10174653

This book is a reproduction of an important historical work. Forgotten Books uses state-of-the-art technology to digitally reconstruct the work, preserving the original format whilst repairing imperfections present in the aged copy. In rare cases, an imperfection in the original, such as a blemish or missing page, may be replicated in our edition. We do, however, repair the vast majority of imperfections successfully; any imperfections that remain are intentionally left to preserve the state of such historical works.

Forgotten Books is a registered trademark of FB &c Ltd.
Copyright © 2018 FB &c Ltd.
FB &c Ltd, Dalton House, 60 Windsor Avenue, London, SW19 2RR.
Company number 08720141. Registered in England and Wales.

For support please visit www.forgottenbooks.com

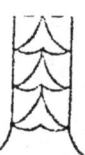

THE M

THE MASQUE OF ANARCHY.

OF THIS BOOK
TWO HUNDRED COPIES ONLY
HAVE BEEN PRINTED

THE

MASQUE OF ANARCHY.

A Poem.

BY PERCY BYSSHE SHELLEY.

TYPE-FAC-SIMILE REPRINT OF

The Original Edition, first published (together with a Preface by Leigh Hunt) in 1832.

Edited

BY THOMAS J. WISE.

London:

PUBLISHED FOR THE SHELLEY SOCIETY

BY REEVES AND TURNER, 196 STRAND.

1892

CONTENTS.

BIBLIOGRAPHY OF: PAGE

    THE FIRST EDITION, 1832 xii

    WATSON'S EDITION, 1842 xiii

    FAC-SIMILE OF SHELLEY'S MANUSCRIPT, EDITED BY H. BUXTON FORMAN xv

    SHELLEY, PETERLOO, AND THE *Mask of Anarchy* xviii

Type-fac-simile reprint.

PREFACE, BY LEIGH HUNT v

TEXT OF THE *MASQUE* 1

BIBLIOGRAPHY.

BIBLIOGRAPHY.

In the autumn of 1819 Shelley was residing at the Villa Valsovano, near Leghorn, and it was here that the tidings of the now famous "Peterloo Massacre," which took place at Manchester on *August 16th*, 1819, reached his ears. The news seems, from the abundant evidence before us, to have filled him with a more than usual amount of horror and disgust, and he at once threw his feelings into words in the lines of *The Masque of Anarchy*. The poem, when completed, was transcribed by Mary Shelley; and this transcript, freely revised by Shelley himself, was forwarded to Leigh Hunt, in England, for insertion in the

Examiner, of which paper Hunt was at that time the Editor. For reasons which may readily be apprehended Hunt deemed it imprudent to print the poem then, and it remained in manuscript until the year 1832, when Moxon issued a slender booklet, of the title-page of which the following is a transcript:

The / Masque of Anarchy. / A Poem. / By Percy Bysshe Shelley. / Now first published, with a Preface / by Leigh Hunt. / Hope is strong; / Justice and Truth their winged child have found. / Revolt of Islam. / London: / Edward Moxon, 64, New Bond Street. / 1832.

Collation:—Foolscap octavo, pp. xxx + 47; consisting of Fly-title (with blank reverse) pp. i—ii; Title-page, as above (with blank reverse) pp. iii—iv; Preface pp. v—xxx; and

Text of the *Masque* pp. 1—47. The imprint (which occurs at the foot of the last page) is: "London : / Bradbury and Evans, Printers, / Bouverie Street." At the end are two pages filled with Moxon's advertisements. Issued in drab boards, with white paper back-label, which reads *Shelley's Masque*. Some later copies were put up in cloth boards of various colours, with the same label up the back.

No second edition of *The Masque of Anarchy* was published until 1842, when a pamphlet appeared bearing the following title-page :—

The / Masque of Anarchy. / To which is added, / Queen Liberty; / Song—To the Men of England. / By Percy Bysshe Shelley. / With a Preface / By Leigh Hunt. / Hope is strong; / Justice and Truth their winged child have found. / Revolt of Islam. / London : / J. Watson, 15, City Road, Finsbury. / 1842.

Collation:—Foolscap octavo, pp. 24; consisting of Title-page, as above (with blank reverse) pp. 1—2; Preface pp. 3—10; and Text of the *Masque* pp. 11—22; of *Queen Liberty* p. 23; and of the *Song* p. 24. The imprint (at the foot of the last page) reads: "J. Watson, Printer, 15, City Road, Finsbury." Issued in plain paper wrappers, which in some examples are yellow, and in others drab. The *brochure* is now of considerable scarcity.

The manuscript sent from Italy, and from which Hunt printed the *Masque* in 1832, was fortunately preserved by him, and in the year 1876 it passed into the possession of Mr. H. Buxton Forman. Until the commencement of 1887 this manuscript remained the chief known authority for the text of the poem; but in the early days of that year an earlier and far more important manuscript was lent by its possessor, Mr. Lewin Bowring, to Mr. F. S. Ellis, at Torquay; and the fact of its existence was communicated by him to *The Athenæum*, in a letter which appeared in that journal for *January* 22*nd*, 1887. This manuscript, Shelley's original holograph, from which Mary Shelley's transcript was probably made, was transferred, within a week or two of its recovery, to the collection of the present Editor. Its importance being at once recognised by the Committee of the Shelley Society it was promptly photo-lithographed, and a *fac-simile* was published, under Mr. Forman's editorial care, in the following volume :—

The / Mask of Anarchy / Written on the occasion of / The Massacre at Manchester / By Percy Bysshe Shelley / Fac-simile / of the /

Holograph Manuscript / with an / Introduction by / H. Buxton Forman / London / Published for the Shelley Society / By Reeves and Turner 196 Strand / 1887.

Collation :—Quarto, pp. xii + 54 + 24 ; consisting of Half-title (with blank reverse) pp. i—ii; Certificate of Issue (with blank reverse) pp. iii—iv; Title-page, as above (with blank reverse) pp. v—vi ; Bibliographical Note * (with blank reverse) pp. vii—viii ; Contents (with blank reverse) pp. ix—x; Fly-title to the Introduction (with blank reverse) pp. xi—xii; Text of the Introduction, pp. 1—52 ; Fly-title to the *Masque* (with blank reverse) pp. 53—54 ; and the *fac-simile* of *The Masque of Anarchy*

---

* This *Note* states that "the following remarks, although written expressly to accompany the present fac-simile of the holograph *Mask of Anarchy*, now in the possession of Mr. Thomas J. Wise, have furnished the substance of a paper read before the Shelley Society on the 9*th* of *February* 1887, and of an article printed in *The Gentleman's Magazine* for *March* 1887 : but the bearings of the manuscript on the text of the poem are dealt with in the ensuing pages more in detail than in the paper or in the article."

24 un-numbered pages; followed by another un-numbered leaf with the imprint upon its recto. Inserted at the end are 8 pages of advertisements of the Shelley Society's Publications, and Mr. Buxton Forman's editions of Shelley and Keats.

Issued in mottled-grey paper boards, lettered both upon the front, and up the back. Five hundred copies were printed, the published price being Ten Shillings.

The textual variations supplied by the holograph will be found dealt with fully in Mr. Forman's Preface; they also furnished material for a lecture delivered by him before the Shelley Society on February 9th, 1887, and printed in the Society's *Transactions* of that year. The lecture was also printed separately in a thin octavo volume having the following Title-page:—

b

Shelley / "Peterloo" / and / "The Mask of Anarchy" / By / H. Buxton Forman / London / Printed for Private Circulation / 1887.

Collation :—Octavo, pp. 29, including Half-title, Title, and Certificate of issue.
Issued in mottled-grey paper boards, lettered both upon the front, and up the back. Twenty-five copies were printed upon Dutch Hand-made paper, and three upon Vellum. A fac-simile of three of the stanzas of the poem (from Mary Shelley's transcript, worked upon by Shelley) were inserted as a frontispiece.

Such is the Bibliography of *The Màsque of Anarchy,* one of the most interesting of Shelley's lesser works, dealing as it does less with poetic art than with matters of public interest; and showing as it also does what the poet's feelings truly were. In its pages we see Shelley not as a visionist enveloped in his dreams—but as a man sympathising with men; not as an Anarchist, stirring up a useless and wasteful strife—but as an able leader urging his followers to a bloodless revolution; bidding them press forward with strength and vigour, but yet "with folded arms and steady eyes" obeying "the laws of their own land."

> "The old laws of England—they
> Whose reverend heads with age are grey,
> Children of a wiser day."

THOMAS J. WISE.

September, 1892.

THE MASQUE OF ANARCHY.

THE
MASQUE OF ANARCHY.

A Poem.

BY PERCY BYSSHE SHELLEY.

NOW FIRST PUBLISHED, WITH A PREFACE

BY LEIGH HUNT.

> Hope is strong;
> Justice and Truth their winged child have found.
> REVOLT OF ISLAM

LONDON:
EDWARD MOXON, 64, NEW BOND STREET.
1832.

PREFACE.

This Poem was written by Mr. Shelley on occasion of the bloodshed at Manchester, in the year 1819. I was editor of the Examiner at that time, and it was sent to me to be inserted or not in that journal, as I thought fit. I did not insert it, because I thought that the public at large had not become sufficiently discerning to do justice to the sincerity and kind-heartedness of the spirit that walked in this flaming robe of verse. His charity was avowedly more than proportionate to his indignation; yet

I thought that even the suffering part of the people, judging, not unnaturally, from their own feelings, and from the exasperation which suffering produces before it produces knowledge, would believe a hundred-fold in his anger, to what they would in his good intention; and this made me fear that the common enemy would take advantage of the mistake to do them both a disservice. Mr. Shelley's writings have since aided the general progress of knowledge in bringing about a wiser period; and an effusion, which would have got him cruelly misrepresented a few years back, will now do unequivocal honour to his memory, and shew every body what a most considerate and kind, as well as fervent heart, the cause of the world has lost.

The poem, though written purposely in a lax and familiar measure, is highly characteristical of the author. It has the usual ardour of his tone, the unbounded sensibility by which he combines the most domestic with the most remote and fanciful images, and the patience, so beautifully checking, and, in fact, produced by, the extreme impatience of his moral feeling. His patience is the deposit of many impatiences, acting upon an equal measure of understanding and moral taste. His wisdom is the wisdom of a heart overcharged with sensibility, acquiring the profoundest notions of justice from the completest sympathy, and at once taking refuge from its pain, and working out its extremest purposes, in the adoption of a stubborn and loving fortitude which neutralizes resistance. His very strokes of humour, while they startle with their extravagance and even ghastliness, cut to the heart with pathos. The fourth and fifth stanzas, for instance, of this Poem, involve an allusion, which becomes affecting from our knowing what he must have felt when he wrote it. It is to his children, who were taken from him by the late Lord Chancellor, under that preposterous law, by which every succeeding age might be made to blush for the tortures inflicted on the opinions of its predecessor.

"Anarchy the Skeleton," riding through the streets, and grinning and bowing on each side of him,

> As well as if his education
> Had cost ten millions to the nation,

is another instance of the union of ludicrousness

with terror. Hope, looking "more like Despair," and laying herself down before his horses' feet to die, is a touching image. The description of the rise and growth of the Public Enlightenment,

> ———— Upborne on wings whose grain
> Was as the light of sunny rain,

and producing "thoughts" as he went,

> As stars from night's loose hair are shaken,

till on a sudden the prostrate multitude look up,

> and ankle-deep in blood,
> Hope, that maiden most serene,
> Was walking with a quiet mien,

is rich with the author's usual treasure of imagery and splendid words. The sixty-third is a delicious stanza, producing a most happy and comforting picture in the midst of visions of blood and tumult. We see the light from its cottage window. The substantial blessings of Freedom are nobly described; and lastly, the advice given by the poet, the great national measure recommended by him, is singularly striking as a *political anticipation*. It advises what has since taken place, and what was felt by the grown wisdom of the age to be the only thing which *could* take place, with effect, as a final rebuke and nullification of the Tories; to wit, a calm, lawful, and inflexible preparation for resistance in the shape of a protesting multitude, — the few against the many,—the laborious and suffering against the spoilt children of monopoly,—Mankind against Tory-kind. It is true the Poet recommends that there should be no active resistance, come what might; which is a piece of fortitude, however effective, which we believe was not contemplated by the Political Unions: yet, in point of the spirit of the thing, the success he anticipates has actually occurred, and after his very fashion; for there really has been no resistance, except by multitudinous protest. The Tories, however desirous they showed themselves to draw their swords, did not draw them. The battle was won without a blow.

Mr. Shelley's countrymen know how anxious he was for the advancement of the common good, but they have yet to become acquainted with his anxiety in behalf of this particular means of it—Reform. The first time I heard from him, was upon the subject: it was before I knew him, and while he was a student at Oxford, in the year 1811. So early did he begin his career of philanthropy! Mankind, and their interests, were scarcely ever out of his thoughts. It was a moot point when he entered your room, whether he would begin with some half-pleasant, half-pensive joke, or quote something Greek, or ask some question about public affairs. I remember his coming upon me when I had not seen him for a long time; and after grappling my hands with both his, in his usual fervent manner, sitting down, and looking at me very earnestly, with a deep though not melancholy interest in his face. We were sitting in a cottage study with our knees to the fire, to which we had been getting nearer and nearer in the comfort of finding ourselves together; the pleasure of seeing him was my only feeling at the moment; and the air of domesticity about us was so complete, that I thought he was going to speak of some family matter—either his or my own; when he asked me, at the close of an intensity of pause, what was "the amount of the National Debt."

I used to rally him on the apparent inconsequentiality of his manner upon these occasions; and he was always ready to carry on the joke, because he said that my laughter did not hinder my being in earnest. With deepest love and admiration was my laughter mixed, or I should not have ventured upon paying him the compliment of it.

I have now before me his corrected proof of an anonymous pamphlet which he wrote in the year 1817, entitled "A Proposal for Putting

Reform to the Vote through the Country." I will make an extract or two from it, to shew how zealous he was on the subject; how generous in the example which he offered to set in behalf of Reform; and how judicious as well as fervent this most calumniated and noble spirit could be in recommending the most avowed of his opinions. The title-page of the proof is scrawled over with sketches of trees and foliage, which was a habit of his in the intervals of thinking, whenever he had pen or pencil in hand. He would indulge in it while waiting for you at an inn, or in a door-way, scratching his elms and oak-trees on the walls. He did them very spiritedly, and with what the painters call a gusto, particularly in point of grace. If he had room, he would add a cottage, and a piece of water, with a sailing boat mooring among the trees. This was his *beau ideal* of a life, the repose of which was to be earned by zeal for his species, and warranted by the common good. What else the image of a boat brings to the memory of those who have lost him, I will not say, especially as he is still with us in his writings. But it is worth observing how agreeably this habit of sketching trees and bowers evinced the gentleness of my friend's nature, the longing he had for rest, and the smallness of his personal desires.

It has been hastily implied in a late notice of him, in a periodical work, that he was an aristocrat by disposition as well as birth; a conclusion natural enough, even with intelligent men, who have been bred among aristocratical influences; but it is a pity that any such persons should give it as their opinion, because it tends to confirm inferior understandings in a similar delusion, and to make the vulgarity of would-be refinement still more confident in its assumptions. It is acknowledged on all hands, that Mr. Shelley's mind was not one to be measured by common rules,—not even by such as the vulgar, great or small, take for uncommon ones, or for cunning pieces of corporate knowledge snugly kept between one another. If there is anything which I can affirm of my beloved friend, with as much confidence as the fact of his being benevolent *and* a friend, it is that he was totally free from mistakes of this kind; that he never for one moment confounded the claims of real and essential, with those of conventional refinement; or allowed one to be substituted for the other in his mind by any compromise of his self-love.

I will admit it to be *possible*, that there were moments in which he might have been deceived in his estimation of people's manners, in consequence of those to which he had been early accustomed; but the charge implied against him involves a conscious, or at least an habitual, preference of what are called high-bred manners, for their own sakes, apart from the natures of those who exhibited them, and to the disadvantage of those to whom they had not been taught. I can affirm that it is a total mistake, and that he partook of no such weakness. I have seen him indeed draw himself up with a sort of irrepressible air of dignified objection, when moral vulgarity was betrayed in his presence, whatever might have been the rank of the betrayer; but nobody could hail with greater joy and simplicity, or meet upon more equal grounds, the instinct of a real delicacy and good intention, come in what shape it might. Why should he have done otherwise? He was Shelley; and not merely a man of that name. What had ordinary high life, and its pretensions, and the getting together of a few people for the sake of giving themselves a little importance, to do with his universal affinities? It was finely said one day in my hearing by Mr. Hazlitt, when asked why he could not temporize a little now and then, or make a compromise with an untruth, that it was "not worth his while." It was not worth Mr. Shelley's while to be an aristocrat. His spirit was large enough to take ten aristocracies into the hollow of his hand, and look at them as I have seen him look at insects from a tree, certainly with no thought either of superiority or the reverse, but with a curious interest.

That quintessence of gentlemanly demeanour which was observable in Mr. Shelley, in drawing-rooms, when he was not over-thoughtful, was nothing but an exquisite combination of sense, moral grace, and habitual sympathy. It was more dignified than what is called dignity in others, because it was the heart of the thing itself, or intrinsic worth, graced by the sincerest idealism; and not a response made by imputed merit to the homage of the imputers. The best conventional dignity could have no more come up to it, than the trick of an occasion to the truth of a life.*

But if an aristocracy of intellect and morals were required, he was the man for one of their

---

* The consciousness of possessing the respect of others, apart from any reason for it but a conventional one, will sometimes produce a really fine expression of countenance, where the nature is good. On the other hand, I have seen Mr. Shelley, from a doubt of the sympathy of those around him, suddenly sink from the happier look above described, into an expression of misgiving and even of destitution, that was extremely touching. It arose out of a sudden impression, that all the sympathy was on his side. Sympathy is undoubtedly the one thing needful and final; and though the receipt of it on false grounds, appears the most formidable obstacle in the way of its true ascendancy, and is so, yet out of the very spirit of that fact will come the salvation of the world; for when once a right view of it gets into fashion, the prejudices as well as understandings of mankind will be as much on that side as they are against it now, and the acceleration of good be without a drawback.

leaders. High and princely was the example he could set to an aristocracy of a different sort, as the reader will see by the following extract from his pamphlet. The late death of an extraordinary man of genius, the delight of nations, and the special glory of his country, has just shewn the blushing world what little things could be done for him, dead or alive, by the "great men" whom he condescended to glorify. The manager of a Scottish theatre (to his immortal credit) * has contributed, in furtherance of the erection of a monument to him, precisely the same sum as was drawn forth out of the money bags of a Scottish

---

* Mr. Murray. I remember the gentlemanly paternity of his father's manner on the English stage, and the fine eyes of his sister (Mrs. Henry Siddons); and was not surprised to find generosity in such a stock.

Duke in the receipt of nearly a thousand pounds a day. The sum is the same that is mentioned in the ensuing paragraph from Mr. Shelley's pamphlet. After proposing a meeting of the Friends of Reform, for the purpose of recommending his plan to the nation, the author notices the expenses which would probably be incurred; and then makes the following offer:—

"I have an income of a thousand a year, on which I support my wife and children in decent comfort, and from which I satisfy certain large claims of general justice.* Should any plan

---

* By these "claims of justice," he meant the wants of his friends and the poor. I do not wish, God knows, to dispute the phrase with him; but such were the notions of this singular "aristocrat," and most equal-sighted fellow-creature.

resembling that which I have proposed be determined on by you, I will give 100*l*., being a tenth part of one year's income, towards its object; and I will not deem so proudly of myself as to believe that I shall stand alone in this respect, when any rational or consistent scheme for the public benefit shall have received the sanction of those great and good men who have devoted themselves for its preservation."

The delight of talking about my friend, has led me into a longer Preface than I intended to write. I did not think of detaining the reader so long from his Poem :—most probably, indeed, I have not detained him. I will, however, make the other, and longer extract, without further remark. If this Pamphlet was the work of an aristocrat, even in the passages where it recommends time to be given for the abolition of his class, he was surely the strangest republican of an aristocrat that ever existed, and had the oddest notions of what was puerile!*

"A certain degree of coalition," says he, "among the sincere friends of Reform, in

---

* See his works, *passim*. A multitude of passages might be quoted, such as no aristocrat would write out of mere spleen, or "with greater pride of his own." They are too frequent, earnest, and full of thought. If Mr. Shelley met with a gird at things aristocratical, in any book he was reading, he marked it as worthy to be noted. I was looking the other day into a Diogenes Laertius that belonged to him, and almost the first passage I met with thus marked, was a saying of the biographer's namesake, in which birth and honours are treated with contempt. I am not here begging the question against such things. I am merely recording my friend's real opinions. The only sentiment by which a privileged class is to be vindicated, may claim a fair discussion; and the settlement of it be safely left to the growth of the sentiment itself, and its expansion into a freedom from its own necessity.

whatever shape, is indispensable to the success of this proposal. The friends of universal or of limited suffrage, of Annual or Triennial Parliaments, ought to settle the subjects on which they disagree, when it is known whether the nation wills that measure on which they are all agreed. It is trivial to discuss what species of Reform should have place, when it yet remains a question whether there will be any Reform or no. Meanwhile, nothing remains for me but to state explicitly my sentiments on this subject. The statement is indeed quite foreign to the merits of the proposal in itself; and I should have suppressed it, until called upon to subscribe such a requisition as I have suggested, if the question which it is natural to ask, as to what are the sentiments of the person who originates the scheme, could have received in any other manner a more simple or direct reply.

"It appears to me, that Annual Parliaments ought to be adopted as an immediate measure, as one which strongly tends to preserve the liberty and happiness of the nation. It would enable men to cultivate those energies on which the performance of the political duties belonging to the citizen of a free state, as the rightful guardian of its prosperity, essentially depends; it would familiarize men with liberty, by disciplining them to an habitual acquaintance with its forms. Political institution is undoubtedly susceptible of such improvements as no rational person can consider possible, so long as the present degraded condition to which the vital imperfections in the existing system of government has reduced the vast multitude of men shall subsist. The securest method of arriving at such beneficial innovations, is to proceed gradually, and with caution; or, in the place of that order and freedom, which the friends of Reform assert to be violated now, anarchy and despotism will follow. Annual Parliaments have my entire assent. I will not state those general reasonings in their favour, which Mr. Cobbett and other writers have already made familiar to the public mind.

"With respect to Universal Suffrage, I confess I consider its adoption, in the present unprepared state of public knowledge and feeling, fraught with peril. I think that none but those who register their names as paying a certain small sum in *direct taxes,** ought, at present, to send Members to Parliament. The consequence of the *immediate* extension of the elective franchise to *every* male adult, would be to place power in the hands of men who have been rendered brutal, and torpid, and ferocious, *by ages of slavery.* It is to suppose that the qualities belonging to a demagogue are such as are sufficient to endow a legislator. I allow Major Cartwright's arguments to be unanswerable; abstractedly it is the right of every human being to have a share in the government. But Mr. Paine's arguments are also unanswerable: *a pure republic may be shewn, by inferences the most obvious and irresistible, to*

---

* His own italics. The rest are the Editor's.

be that system of social order the fittest to produce the happiness, and promote the genuine eminence of man. Yet nothing can be less consistent with reason, or afford smaller hopes of any beneficial issue, than the plan which should abolish the regal and the aristocratical branches of our constitution, *before the public mind,* through many gradations of improvement, shall have arrived at the maturity which can *disregard those symbols of its childhood.*"

I need not point out to the reader's attention the singular and happy anticipations contained in the above extract; neither shall I stop to inquire how far Mr. Shelley would have thought the feasibilities of improvement hastened by the events that have taken place of late years— events, one of them in particular, (the Glorious

Three Days) which it would have repaid him for all his endurances, had he lived to see.

And who shall say that he has not seen them? For if ever there was a man upon earth, of a more spiritual nature than ordinary, partaking of the errors and perturbations of his species, but seeing and working through them with a seraphical purpose of good, such an one was Percy Bysshe Shelley.

L. H.

THE
MASQUE OF ANARCHY.

I.

As I lay asleep in Italy,

There came a voice from over the sea,

And with great power it forth led me

To walk in the visions of Poesy.

II.

I met Murder on the way—

He had a mask like Castlereagh—

Very smooth he look'd, yet grim;

Seven bloodhounds followed him:

III.

All were fat; and well they might

Be in admirable plight,

For one by one, and two by two,

He tossed them human hearts to chew,

Which from his wide cloak he drew.

IV.

Next came Fraud, and he had on,

Like Lord E——, an ermined gown;

His big tears, for he wept well,

Turned to mill-stones as they fell;

V.

And the little children, who

Round his feet played to and fro,

Thinking every tear a gem,

Had their brains knocked out by them.

THE MASQUE OF ANARCHY.

VI.

Clothed with the * * as with light,

And the shadows of the night,

Like * * * next, Hypocrisy,

On a crocodile rode by.

VII.

And many more Destructions played

In this ghastly masquerade,

All disguised, even to the eyes,

Like bishops, lawyers, peers, or spies.

VIII.

Last came Anarchy; he rode

On a white horse, splashed with blood;

He was pale even to the lips,

Like Death in the Apocalypse.

IX.

And he wore a kingly crown;

And in his grasp a sceptre shone;

And on his brow this mark I saw—

"I am God, and King, and Law!"

X.

With a pace stately and fast,

Over English land he past,

Trampling to a mire of blood

The adoring multitude.

XI.

And a mighty troop around,

With their trampling shook the ground,

Waving each a bloody sword,

For the service of their Lord.

THE MASQUE OF ANARCHY.

XII.

And with glorious triumph, they

Rode through England proud and gay,

Drunk as with intoxication

Of the wine of desolation.

XIII.

O'er fields and towns, from sea to sea,

Passed the pageant swift and free,

Tearing up, and trampling down,

Till they came to London town.

XIV.

And each dweller, panic-stricken,

Felt his heart with terror sicken,

Hearing the tempestuous cry

Of the triumph of Anarchy.

XV.

For with pomp to meet him came,

Clothed in arms like blood and flame,

The hired murderers who did sing,

" Thou art God, and Law, and King.

XVI.

"We have waited, weak and lone,

For thy coming, Mighty One!

Our purses are empty, our swords are cold,

Give us glory, and blood, and gold."

XVII.

Lawyers and priests, a motley crowd,

To the earth their pale brows bowed;

Like a bad prayer not over loud,

Whispering—"Thou art Law and God."

XVIII.

Then all cried with one accord,

"Thou art King, and God, and Lord;

Anarchy, to thee we bow,

Be thy name made holy now!"

XIX.

And Anarchy, the skeleton,

Bowed and grinned to every one,

As well as if his education,

Had cost ten millions to the nation.

XX.

For he knew the palaces

Of our kings were nightly his;

His the sceptre, crown, and globe,

And the gold-in-woven robe.

XXI.

So he sent his slaves before

To seize upon the Bank and Tower,

And was proceeding with intent

To meet his pensioned parliament,

XXII.

When one fled past, a maniac maid,

And her name was Hope, she said:

But she looked more like Despair;

And she cried out in the air;

XXIII.

" My father, Time, is weak and grey

With waiting for a better day;

See how idiot-like he stands,

Fumbling with his palsied hands!

XXIV.

"He has had child after child,

And the dust of earth is piled

Over every one but me—

Misery! oh, Misery!"

XXV.

Then she lay down in the street,

Right before the horses' feet,

Expecting with a patient eye,

Murder, Fraud, and Anarchy.

XXVI.

When between her and her foes

A mist, a light, an image rose,

Small at first, and weak and frail

Like the vapour of the vale:

XXVII.

Till, as clouds grow on the blast,

Like tower-crown'd giants striding fast,

And glare with lightnings as they fly,

And speak in thunder to the sky,

XXVIII.

It grew—a shape arrayed in mail

Brighter than the viper's scale,

And upborne on wings whose grain

Was as the light of sunny rain.

XXIX.

On its helm, seen far away,

A planet, like the morning's, lay;

And those plumes it light rained through,

Like a shower of crimson dew.

XXX.

With step as soft as wind it passed

O'er the heads of men—so fast

That they knew the presence there,

And looked—and all was empty air.

XXXI.

As flowers beneath the footstep waken,

As stars from night's loose hair are shaken,

As waves arise when loud winds call,

Thoughts sprung where'er that step did fall.

XXXII.

And the prostrate multitude

Looked—and ankle deep in blood,

Hope, that maiden most serene,

Was walking with a quiet mien:

XXXIII.

And Anarchy, the ghastly birth,

Lay dead earth upon the earth;

The Horse of Death, tameless as wind,

Fled, and with his hoofs did grind

To dust the murderers thronged behind.

XXXIV.

A rushing light of clouds and splendour,

A sense, awakening and yet tender,

Was heard and felt—and at its close

These words of joy and fear arose:

XXXV.

(As if their own indignant earth,

Which gave the sons of England birth,

Had felt their blood upon her brow,

And shuddering with a mother's throe,

XXXVI.

Had turned every drop of blood,

By which her face had been bedewed,

To an accent unwithstood,

As if her heart had cried aloud :)

XXXVII.

" Men of England, Heirs of Glory,

Heroes of unwritten story,

Nurslings of one mighty mother,

Hopes of her, and one another,

XXXVIII.

" Rise, like lions after slumber,

In unvanquishable number,

Shake your chains to earth like dew,

Which in sleep had fall'n on you.

XXXIX.

" What is Freedom ?   Ye can tell

That which Slavery is too well,

For its very name has grown

To an echo of your own.

XL.

" 'Tis to work, and have such pay

As just keeps life from day to day

In your limbs, as in a cell

For the tyrants' use to dwell:

XLI.

" So that ye for them are made,

Loom, and plough, and sword, and spade;

With or without your own will, bent

To their defence and nourishment.

XLII.

" Tis to see your children weak

With their mothers pine and peak,

When the winter winds are bleak:—

They are dying whilst I speak.

XLIII.

" 'Tis to hunger for such diet,

As the rich man in his riot

Casts to the fat dogs that lie

Surfeiting beneath his eye.

XLIV.

" 'Tis to let the Ghost of Gold

Take from toil a thousand fold,

More than e'er its substance could

In the tyrannies of old:

XLV.

" Paper coin—that forgery

Of the title deeds, which ye

Hold to something of the worth

Of the inheritance of Earth.

XLVI.

" 'Tis to be a slave in soul,

And to hold no strong controul

Over your own wills, but be

All that others make of ye.

XLVII.

" And at length when ye complain,

With a murmur weak and vain,

'Tis to see the tyrant's crew

Ride over your wives and you :—

Blood is on the grass like dew.

XLVIII.

" Then it is to feel revenge,

Fiercely thirsting to exchange

Blood for blood—and wrong for wrong:

DO NOT THUS, WHEN YE ARE STRONG.

XLIX.

" Birds find rest in narrow nest,

When weary of the winged quest;

Beasts find fare in woody lair,

When storm and snow are in the air.

L.

"Asses, swine, have litter spread,

And with fitting food are fed;

All things have a home but one:

Thou, oh Englishman, hast none!

LI.

"This is Slavery—savage men,

Or wild beasts within a den,

Would endure not as ye do:

But such ills they never knew.

LII.

"What art thou, Freedom? Oh! could Slaves

Answer from their living graves

This demand, tyrants would flee

Like a dream's dim imagery.

LIII.

"Thou art not, as impostors say,

A shadow soon to pass away,

A superstition, and a name

Echoing from the caves of Fame.

LIV.

"For the labourer thou art bread,

And a comely table spread,

From his daily labour come,

In a neat and happy home.

LV.

"Thou art clothes, and fire, and food

For the trampled multitude:

No—in countries that are free

Such starvation cannot be,

As in England now we see.

LVI.

"To the rich thou art a check,

When his foot is on the neck

Of his victim; thou dost make

That he treads upon a snake.

LVII.

' Thou art Justice—ne'er for gold

May thy righteous laws be sold,

As laws are in England :—thou

Shield'st alike the high and low.

LVIII.

"Thou art Wisdom—Freedom never

Dreams that God will damn for ever

All who think those things untrue,

Of which priests make much ado.

LIX.

"Thou art Peace—never by thee

Would blood and treasure wasted be,

As tyrants wasted them, when all

Leagued to quench thy flame in Gaul.

LX.

" What if English toil and blood

Was poured forth, even as a flood!

It availed,—oh Liberty!

To dim—but not extinguish thee.

LXI.

" Thou art Love—the rich have kist

Thy feet, and like him following Christ,

Give their substance to the free,

And through the rough world follow thee.

LXII.

"Oh turn their wealth to arms, and make

War for thy beloved sake,

On wealth *and* war and fraud: whence they

Drew the power which is their prey.

LXIII.

" Science, and Poetry, and Thought,

Are thy lamps; they make the lot

Of the dwellers in a cot

So serene, they curse it not.

LXIV.

" Spirit, Patience, Gentleness,

All that can adorn and bless,

Art thou : let deeds, not words, express

Thine exceeding loveliness.

LXV.

" Let a great assembly be

Of the fearless, of the free,

On some spot of English ground,

Where the plains stretch wide around.

LXVI.

"Let the blue sky overhead,

The green earth, on which ye tread,

All that must eternal be,

Witness the solemnity.

LXVII.

"From the corners uttermost

Of the bounds of English coast;

From every hut, village, and town,

Where those who live and suffer, moan

For others' misery and their own:

LXVIII.

"From the workhouse and the prison,

Where pale as corpses newly risen,

Women, children, young, and old,

Groan for pain, and weep for cold;

LXIX.

"From the haunts of daily life,

Where is waged the daily strife

With common wants and common cares,

Which sow the human heart with tares;

LXX.

"Lastly, from the palaces,

Where the murmur of distress

Echoes, like the distant sound

Of a wind alive around;

LXXI.

"Those prison-halls of wealth and fashion,

Where some few feel such compassion

For those who groan, and toil, and wail,

As must make their brethren pale;

LXXII.

"Ye who suffer woes untold,

Or to feel, or to behold

Your lost country bought and sold

With a price of blood and gold;

LXXIII.

"Let a vast assembly be,

And with great solemnity

Declare with measured words, that ye

Are, as God has made ye, free !

LXXIV.

"Be your strong and simple words

Keen to wound as sharpened swords,

And wide as targes let them be,

With their shade to cover ye.

LXXV.

"Let the tyrants pour around

With a quick and startling sound,

Like the loosening of a sea,

Troops of armed emblazonry.

LXXVI.

" Let the charged artillery drive,

Till the dead air seems alive

With the clash of clanging wheels,

And the tramp of horses' heels.

LXXVII.

" Let the fixed bayonet

Gleam with sharp desire to wet

Its bright point in English blood,

Looking keen as one for food.

LXXVIII.

"Let the horsemen's scimitars

Wheel and flash, like sphereless stars,

Thirsting to eclipse their burning

In a sea of death and mourning.

LXXIX.

"Stand ye calm and resolute,

Like a forest close and mute,

With folded arms, and looks which are

Weapons of an unvanquished war.

LXXX.

"And let Panic, who outspeeds

The career of armed steeds,

Pass, a disregarded shade,

Thro' your phalanx undismay'd.*

---

* The three stanzas next ensuing are printed in italics, not because they are better, or indeed so well written, as some of the rest, but as marking out the sober, lawful, and charitable mode of proceeding advocated and anticipated by this supposed reckless innovator. "*Passive obedience*" he certainly had not; but here follows a picture and a recommendation of "*non-resistance,*" in all its glory. The mingled emotion and dignity of it is admirably expressed in the second line of stanza eighty-five. Let churches militant read it, and blush to call the author no Christian!

LXXXI.

" Let the laws of your own land,

Good or ill, between ye stand,

Hand to hand, and foot to foot,

Arbiters of the dispute.

LXXXII.

" The old laws of England—they

Whose reverend heads with age are grey,

Children of a wiser day;

And whose solemn voice must be

Thine own echo—Liberty!

LXXXIII.

" On those who first should violate

Such sacred heralds in their state,

Rest the blood that must ensue,

And it will not rest on you.

LXXXIV.

" And if then the tyrants dare,

Let them ride among you there;

Slash, and stab, and maim, and hew;

What they like, that let them do.

LXXXV.

"With folded arms and steady eyes,

And little fear and less surprise,

Look upon them as they stay

Till their rage has died away:

LXXXVI.

"Then they will return with shame,

To the place from which they came,

And the blood thus shed will speak

In hot blushes on their cheek:

LXXXVII.

" Every woman in the land

Will point at them as they stand—

They will hardly dare to greet

Their acquaintance in the street:

LXXXVIII.

" And the bold, true warriors,

Who have hugged Danger in wars,

Will turn to those who would be free

Ashamed of such base company:

LXXXIX.

"And that slaughter to the nation

Shall steam up like inspiration,

Eloquent, oracular,

A volcano heard afar:

XC.

"And these words shall then become

Like Oppression's thundered doom,

Ringing through each heart and brain,

Heard again—again—again.

XCI.

Rise like lions after slumber

In unvanquishable NUMBER!

Shake your chains to earth, like dew

Which in sleep had fall'n on you:

YE ARE MANY—THEY ARE FEW.

THE END.

LONDON:
BRADBURY AND EVANS, PRINTERS,
BOUVERIE STREET.

WS - #0035 - 180923 - C0 - 229/152/6 [8] - CB - 9780266569701 - Gloss Lamination